This book belongs to

_____

_____

_____

First published in Great Britain in 2020

Society for Promoting Christian Knowledge, 36 Causton Street, London SW1P 4ST
www.spck.org.uk

Illustrations © Jean Claude 2020

British Library Cataloguing-in-Publication Data
A catalogue record for this book is available from the British Library

ISBN 978–0–281–08121–9

1 3 5 7 9 10 8 6 4 2

Printed in China by Imago
Subsequently digitally printed in Great Britain

Produced on paper from sustainable forests

AWAY
in a
MANGER

Illustrated by Jean Claude

spck

Away in a manger,

no crib for a bed,

the little Lord Jesus
laid down his sweet head.

The stars in the bright sky

looked down
where he lay,

the little Lord Jesus,
asleep on the hay.

The cattle are lowing,
the baby awakes,

but little Lord Jesus
no crying he makes.

I love thee, Lord Jesus!
Look down from the sky.

and stay by my side until
morning is nigh.

Be near me,
Lord Jesus;

I ask thee to stay

close by me for ever, and love me, I pray.

Bless all the dear children in thy tender care,

and fit us for heaven,

to live with thee there.